Cuoreosity

The heArt of Being

Jamie Millard

Dedication

ΓΝΩΘΙ ΣΑΥΤΟΝ

"Know Thyself" was carved into stone at the entrance to Apollo's temple at Delphi in Greece.

Odysseus cried and Pericles rolled in his grave as my grandfather, Demetre Politis, sailed away from Piraeus, Greece in 1953 to start over again in Canada. His risks became my rewards. A spellbinder, I was raised on his knee to the exploits of Aphrodite, Hercules, Helen, Leonidas, Medusa and Perseus. He brought their stories and their adventures so vividly to life, yet he was always my real hero. He taught me to listen deeply, to ask questions, to speak wisely and to tell my own story. Never to search for myself but to find myself. Thank you Papouli for the gift of words and the wings of possibility.

Foreword

On the Wings of Words

Poetry was our first language. Our ear tuned to the soothing iambic pentameter of our mother's beating heart. The preverbal rhythm of nursery rhymes and lullabies known across every culture. Poetry set to music as song. Poetry is the very bridge between music and language. Poetry is music with meaning! Deep and powerful meaning!

German researcher Eugen Wassiliwizky says "Dating back some 4300 years, written poetry is the most ancient record of human literature. The roots of poetry are likely to reach even much further into the past, to a time when literacy had not yet evolved, and poems were passed down in oral traditions. The fact that poetry has accompanied humankind over such a long period suggests a strong grip on human cognition and emotion."

As Pablo Neruda confesses, "Poetry arrives in search of us. I don't know where it came from, from winter or a river. I don't know how or when." Poetry has always been a part of us!

Cognitive neuroscientist Guillame Thierry found," the brain is hardwired for poetry. Poetry appears to be 'built-in,' it is like a profound intuition, every human being is an unconscious poet."

The emotional often invisible unconscious power of poetry nourishes our intuition, wisdom, and awareness to shape our interoception. This so-called sixth sense dances with our deep insights at the intersection of our emotions, thoughts, and bodily sensations. Interoception may be the seat of spirituality. The portal to source. Poetry may be knocking on the very door to our soul.

Poetry expresses what mere conversation cannot do. When we write, we can be anybody and anything! When we write, we are everything. When we write we can be our own authentic self. When we write we are free! Words can free us. Words can help us learn to forgive. Words can heal us.

Emily Dickinson declared, "I know nothing in the world that has as much power as a word. Sometimes I write one, and I look at it, until it begins to shine." A word only beginning to live as it is set free. One word has infinite possibilities. Only one word.

In, "I Dwell in Possibility", her poem about poetry as compared to prose, Dickinson states that poetry itself opens windows and doors to more spacious, sacred, and deeper possibilities.

Poetry is a crack in the armour of fear.

According to Kim Rosen "Poetry, the most ancient form of prayer, is a necessary medicine for our times: a companion through difficulty; a guide when we are lost; a salve when we are wounded; and a conduit to an inner source of joy, freedom, and insight."

Rosen states "Through poetry, the unspeakable can be spoken, the unendurable endured, and the miraculous shared."

Mary Oliver sharing that, "Poetry is a life-cherishing force. For poems are not words, after all, but fires for the cold, ropes let down to the lost, something as necessary as bread in the pockets of the hungry."

Poetry can save lives.

If great poetry is anything, it is great storytelling. The way we tell our stories has a lot to do with the way we see ourselves in the world, with our identity. Poetry is both shelter and the storm. It validates us and it possesses us! It holds us. It challenges us. Poetry changes us!

Poetry has a consciousness all of its own. T. S. Eliot famously stated that "genuine poetry can communicate before it is understood".

Thierry confers with Eliot admitting that "Sometimes when you read a poem, you feel that somehow something has changed. It's a bit like a crack in the ice, like okay, this is a change of paradigm, there was a before and an after to when I've read this. And now I see the world differently."

Poetry moves us! Poetry touches us somewhere in the bittersweet place between suffering and pleasure. Wassiliwizky and his team showed that poetry is capable of inducing peak emotional experiences often accompanied by chills and goosebumps. Poetry-elicited chills differed from those evoked by music pointing to the unique qualities of poetic language that could not be replaced by music and singing during the evolution of human forms of emotional expression. Poetry represents an ancient, cross-cultural, and emotionally powerful variety within the human communicative and expressive repertoire.

Neruda talks of being possessed by poetry. Words finding him. Words writing themselves as he is swallowed by a sense of oneness with the universe. Wheeling with the stars. His heart broken loose on the wind! His soul ignited. Awakening with a poem.

Poetry is alive as a river of magical vibration that lets love and light flow deep into our body, dancing with our spirit to give birth to a stranger that we get to fall in love with all over again. Ourselves.

Poetry is an invitation to questions whose answers we will become.

In a 1903 letter to his protégé, the 19-year-old cadet and budding poet Franz Xaver Kappus, the poet Rainer Maria Rilke writes: "I want to beg you, as much as I can, dear sir, to be patient toward all that is unsolved in your heart and to try to love the questions themselves like locked rooms and like books that are written in a very foreign tongue. Do not now seek the answers, which cannot be given you because you would not be able to live them. And the point is, to live everything. Live the questions now. Perhaps you will then gradually, without noticing it, live along some distant day into the answer."

Without preconceived answers, there is eloquence and beauty in one's questions, living themselves out in ever broadening circles. There is no answer in the strictest sense. What emerges in the silence are new questions and as Rilke said, "We live into the questions."

David Whyte calls them the questions that have patiently waited for us. The questions that have no right to go away! The transformative stirrings that have to do with the person we are about to become. The poetry of solace.

Mary Oliver decreeing that the questions themselves make music and nourish us. Life after all is a mystery! John O'Donohue stated, "It's strange to be here. The mystery never leaves you."

Each of our lives is a poem in itself. A rhythm. We live between breaths, between heartbeats, between dark and light, day and night, between visible and invisible, stimulus and response, between feeling and emotion, known and mystery, between fact and possibility, conscious and unconscious, choice and action, between courage and regret, listening and speaking, warm and cold, between art and science, desire and faith, between reacting and creating, and between love and fear. Between thought and expression lies a lifetime. Poetry is a portal into our shadows. It is the emancipation of our spirit as it engages in a deeper conversation with our soul. Poetry is a threshold to our own often silenced voice as it searches for meaning and purpose.

Empathy, compassion, imagination, and creativity all whirling with the very source that connects us with everything.

Our whole being is engaged in this conversation, way beyond just an exchange of information. Poetry guides us to "divine" meaning as opposed to define meaning! Being as opposed to doing. We are after all human beings.

Cuoreosity is an invitation into this heArt of Being. An invitation to our soul.

Poetry is a bridge to love itself. Love is innate to us all but is often forgotten in its current hijacked Hollywood presentation. Love transcends our communication, taking it to a higher level. In this magical place of parable and poetry, our whole being is engaged in communication. It changes the writer, listener, and reader. We cannot leave this place untouched. We feel a deeper connection with ourselves. We feel a deeper connection to the world and to the source beyond. A oneness.

We are according to John O'Donohue, "a body in a soul".

We are souls having a human experience.

As Rumi eloquently professes "Out beyond ideas of wrongdoing and right doing, there is a field. I'll meet you there. When the soul lies down in that grass, the world is too full to talk about. Ideas, language, even the phrase 'each other' doesn't make any sense."

Poetry is the meditative language of the moment! Poetry is the language of our soul. The very language of transcendence itself. Awareness.

The longest journey we will ever make is the forty-five cm or eighteen inches from our head to our heart to our soul! This door only opens from the inside! We are the sanctuary, as Rumi exclaims.

Poetry is an angel of forgiveness that opens up our heart and guides us to the very door to our soul.

We have to pull it open and be brave enough to take the only step we can. The one towards our "self".

On the wings of words
May you be Cuoreous!
Opening your heArt of Being
Walking beside the Grace of mystery
As she collides with your spirit
May the consciousness of words
invite you into a deeper conversation
with the very voice
that aches in your bones
On the wings of words
May you connect to the river of awe that
swims inside of everything
transcending your senses
A body in a soul
Flowing in oneness
with the universe

An ocean of awareness
walking with possibility
May you feel the invitation of truth
kissing the divine hand of time
On the wings of words
May you live your questions
May poetry arrive to find you
as shelter and a storm
May you meet the authenticity of your soul
greeting the very stranger you are becoming
May you fall in love with yourself
all over again
On the wings of words
May you open the door
and cross the threshold
Home

Thank you for reading!
Jamie Millard
London, Canada
May 2022

Contents

Introduction

I WAS TWELVE when the words found me. Poetry arrived in search of me. I don't know where it came from. I don't know how. I was in a hospital neurology ward being investigated for a possible brain tumour or aneurysm due to the sudden onset of some very bizarre sensory changes and a severe headache. In the more limited diagnostic reality of 1980, with a spinal tap and an angiogram under my belt, it seemed that I had inherited an odd form of ancestral migraine with a spectacular aura that demanded the limelight as it announced its arrival. With this new invitation to breathe again, I was allowed to get up to walk for the first time in days. My head throbbing, held up only by the delicate wobble of sailor's legs, I explored the brave new world of the hallway corridor being drawn to the large window at the very end. As I got closer, I saw him. A boy about my age. Sitting quietly and staring out the window. His head was shaved. A fresh incision with stitches weaved a winding track over his skull. Our eyes met. In what I now know was a moment of love, a poem had come calling. I went back to the room and akin to Neruda, I picked up a pencil and I set the words free.

The words wrote themselves as if my hand was not my own. The last lines still fresh in my essence as an invitation to a new story. "Life is more good than bad and I had taken for granted all that I had." The deeper wisdom of awareness and intuition as interoception was trying to speak to the body and mind of a scared twelve-year-old boy. I had crossed a threshold that moment and had entered a portal through the angel of poetry. Looking back now I still get goosebumps as I realize I had opened the door to my soul.

As John O' Donohue professes in Anam Cara, "Once the soul awakens the search begins and you can never go back." Speaking to our own creative expectations he states, "The way you look at things is the most powerful force in shaping your life." Our stories matter. Are we reacting or creating? The letters are the same, but the journey is a much different experience. These two conscious messengers collided in that moment, and I felt something had changed! Much like Neruda's poetic awakening, I heard the voice of my soul speaking the cosmic universal tongue of source through poetry. I had connected to Grace! Grace in my writing represents the universe, source, God, awareness, awen, awe, divine consciousness, the mysterious vital force that connects everything to everything. Spirituality. Non duality. That which unites all things in interdependence. Love!

My peripatetic epiphany had begun. At twelve I did not realize then, that I still had a first mountain to climb. In his book "The Second Mountain", David Brooks says our life story resembles the shape of two mountains. The first mountain is about ego and a vision of prominence, pleasure, and success. A journey dressed in the conditions that were often placed upon us. The first mountain of life is "I am what the world says I am." Brooks stating that the first mountain is about acquisition. We conquer the first mountain. We get to the top and realize a deeper need still calls from aching bones. The second mountain pulls us up. Something calls us to the top in a way Franciscan priest and writer Richard Rohr describes the second half of life as "falling upwards".

Rather than a Hero's Journey, it is more so a Soul Journey. More inwards and deeper, circular yet fractal, less individual and more diversely community. Psychologist, mythologist, and author Sharon Blackie calling it a post heroic journey stating, "Its not about slaying the dragon, but about harnessing his special skills and making him part of the team". Transformation of ourselves and of the world around us. If the first mountain is the safety of our ego, the second is the song of our soul. Individual to interdependence. The transcendence of self. Me to We. Head to heart. Heart to soul.

It's never too early to get knocked off our first mountain. Brooks says it can happen from eight to eighty-five. I stepped off the path at twelve to enjoy the view. It ended up being a brief stop. I climbed slower for six years. The deeper words finding me, and I set them free. I kept them secret as the aesthetics of a male poet did not resonate with the community of fellow mountaineers that were providing for and equipping my journey. High school poetry and the enthusiastic compelling English teacher Ian Underhill, an angel in disguise helped me to understand the gift of the words more passionately. Interestingly the migraines stopped at eighteen and the black and white well paid safe factual world of science won the day over the unpredictable mysterious life of a writer poet.

I was back climbing that first mountain for thirty more years. My ego had done its job well! I climbed to conquer. Higher and higher. Living from my head. At forty-eight, the headaches returned and astonishingly so did the words. Coincidence? I now know not. The poetry arrived to find me at the top of a mountain. She said stop climbing. Sit. Breathe. Believe. I looked out and as the foggy mist lifted into a bright sadness, I found myself looking across a valley at a different mountain. The beautiful questions Rilke, Whyte and Mary Oliver had spoken of had come to feed me. I got knocked off the first mountain by a heavy gale of poetry! I fell upwards!

The second mountain had found me. Poetry had arrived once again. The words now so much louder. At times coming as songs. I didn't know where they came from. I didn't know how. The questions that had patiently waited were now very demanding, loud, and persistent. The words came as a flood of arrival. I just set them free. Was it the fabled mid life or developmental crisis of psychology coined in the 1960s by my fellow Canadian, psychologist Elliot Jacque? It did not feel like a crisis at all. It felt like going home in a sense. A rewarding dance of self growth and self realization. Psychologist Abraham Maslow referred to it as self actualization. I opened this gift. The very present itself. A spiritual awakening!

The existential psychologist John Welwood's poetry captured this awareness so beautifully.

Forget about enlightenment.
Sit down wherever you are
And listen to the wind singing in your veins.
Feel the love, the longing, the fear in your bones.
Open your heart to who you are, right now,
Not who you would like to be,
Not the saint you are striving to become,

But the being right here before you, inside you, around you.
All of you is holy.
You are already more and less
Than whatever you can know.
Breathe out,
Touch in,
Let go.

Singer-songwriter, poet, and novelist, Leonard Cohen sang, "There is a crack, a crack in everything that's how the light gets in." Rumi, who like Rilke, always seems to get there first, professed "The wound is the place where the light enters you." Yes, the light was getting in. I could feel it illuminating the dark corners of my being revealing the shadows that had been hidden to me. I will propose that the light also needs to get out too! What we seek is seeking us as Rumi shared. The light is love. Love seeks us as we seek love. My heart was opening. My soul was speaking and singing. There is an old Sioux saying, "The longest journey we will ever make is from our head to our heart." The second mountain was pulling me up its slope! I was flow-ting. The door only opened from the inside. I had found the handle. I pulled the door open, crossed the threshold and took the only step that I could take. The one towards my authentic self.

Live the questions! Voltaire famously said, "Judge a person by their questions rather than their answers." David Whyte echoing, "If you want a beautiful life start asking beautiful questions." Our individual lives are defined by raw, aching, open questions. The ones that have no right to go away, according to Whyte. Asking a beautiful question starts to shape our identity as much by asking it, as it does by having it answered. We must live the questions, here and now. Gradually without noticing it we will blossom into the answers as Rilke revealed. As we look back on our lives, we will see that the questions themselves were what shaped us all along. The questions are the journey.

Spirituality and creativity appear to intersect as dance partners on my heart and soul journey. The questions demanding to be soothed by that elusive answer to the meaning of life, stimulating another question and lesson on the way to an awakening within my true being. We all encounter the sacred at times in our lives. Awe! A feeling of wonder experienced when facing something greater than the self and beyond current understanding. A newborn child. Nature. Forests. A morning sunrise kissing the beauty of the patiently fading light of a full moon. The ocean. Thresholds. Lost in the moment of the here and the now. Time standing still as we transcend the self and connect to Grace. The words arriving to find me as a beautiful blessing of poetic expression as I live the questions!

Speaking of walking and waking to this wonder, John O'Donohue suggests "I would love to live like a river flows, carried by the surprise of its own unfolding." This state of "flow" leads to creative experiences transcending even time herself. Psychologist Mihaly Csikszentmihalyi, stating "Poetry is about slowing down, I think. It's about reading the same thing again and again, really savoring it, living inside the poem. There's no rush to find out what happens in a poem. It's really about feeling one syllable rubbing against another, one word giving way to another, and sensing the justice of that relationship between one word, the next, the next, the next." Poetry is a portal into that state of flow for me.

Unlike prose, poetry asks us to pay attention to language, word by word, and syllable by syllable. The rhythms of poetry, the lines, and the pauses that are built into the reading experience, slows us down. Poetry asks us to listen deeper and demands presence. This slowing down, this act of awareness and presence itself is a sacred act akin to a meditative prayer. Mindfulness. Poetry opens into the space between things and in turn touches spiritual places inside of us that leads to transformative change.

In that solitude, stillness, and silence I hear the voice of my own soul calling me to a deeper sense of purpose. David Whyte echoing, that "Poetry is the art of overhearing ourselves say things from which it is impossible to retreat!" Poetry speaks loudest to me and through me in the ritualistic quiet of the sweet darkness of dawn as the sun arrives to slowly kiss the moon. Fueled by coffee and the gratitude of a new day, the words come to find me in this harvest of Grace. I meet a stranger each morning in the mirror as I awake. With an open heart and a pen in hand, poetry finds me, and I create in the arms of possibility. A child on Christmas morning! Breathing deeply into the colours of dawn, all of me whole. A presence of wonder. A body in a soul. My very essence guiding me, writing through me, and singing with me. Transcendence of self. This poem that I wrote is an invitation to meet that stranger as a soul.

I hear you loudest
In the silence
Between your words
In the stillness
Between your heartbeats
In the sweet surrender
of what brings you solitude
I hear you loudest
When I meet you
as a soul

According to Maslow, beyond actualization, self transcendence represents the most holistic level of higher consciousness. It is a transpersonal or spiritual dimension defined by connectedness and sacredness. Researcher Scott Kaufman taking Maslow's concept beyond a hierarchy and suggesting that this transformative journey up the second mountain goes beyond the "self". Kaufman suggests that this journey of growth winds through purpose, exploration, and love.

We are all on a journey that explores purpose. We often start this journey on an intellectual path till through real eyes, we realize it is a spiritual journey as University of Santa Monica founders Mary and Ron Hulnick exclaim with a soul line as opposed to a goal line. They share this process so beautifully in their book Remembering the Light Within. We will come full circle from a state of interdependence to individualism and back to divine interdependence again. We wake up to what has always been and what will always be, and what is always eternally present. This sentiment of journey is so beautifully expressed by TS Eliot in Little Gidding".

We shall not cease from exploration
And at the end of all our exploring
Will be to arrive where we started
And know the place for the first time.

That place is love. We wake up to love. The circle of life may just be our journey from head to heart, to soul. The circle of our soul. Coming home to love!

British psychologist, coach and author Robert Holden so beautifully writes about this in his book "Loveability". Love connects us back to our inner child.

In our Instagram frenzied lives, we tend to forget love. We do not lose it. The path back to the clarity of love is a process of subtraction as opposed to addition, as we remove layers and veils that we have worn as armour. The shift from fear to love is the miracle of our lives. Love is our destiny! Our relationship to love affects every relationship in our life, especially the one with our "self".

Love is innate. Love is not a feeling. Holden proclaims, "Love is an intelligence! All beings carry the knowledge of creation in the cells of their body!" We are love! When we tune in to love, love will show us how to live. Love will show us how to love. Love will show us how to create. Holden says, "Love is the heart of our life." Love lives in oneness. Our old "self" does not survive love as on the wings of joy and bliss, love arrives to show us who we really are.

Joseph Campbell said "People say that what we're all seeking is a meaning for life. I don't think that's what we're really seeking. I think that what we're seeking is an experience of being alive, so that our life experiences on the purely physical plane will have resonance within our innermost being and reality, so that we actually feel the rapture of being alive." The rapture of being alive is the journey to our inner being. The journey to our soul. The brilliant poet Tanya Markul giving me chills as she writes, "Miracles don't happen by chance. They happen when you step into the flames that burn your soul."

The word for heart in Italian is "Cuore". The suffix, "osity", reflects "the quality of being." I felt that this soul burning experience of and to aliveness needed its own name. The word **Cuoreosity** found me and captures the essence of this journey guided by love and the mystery of living the questions. The title of this book celebrates this spiritual awakening at the poetic threshold that intersects curiosity, love, and the essence of our innermost being. The journey inwards. Head to Heart to Soul. Purpose, exploration and coming home to love.

About This Book

Cuoreosity. The heArt of Being.

Cuoreosity, the heArt of Being is my first collection of poetry. Cuoreosity is the harvest of this lyrical poetic transcendent journey from my head to my heart to my soul. A spiritual awakening. My spiritual awakening. Over the past seven years these words arrived dancing alongside the beautiful questions that had no right to go away. Poetry found me on the beautiful wings of words. I now set these words free.

This book is organized into three sections of poetry. Each poem is accompanied by a commentary on the following page. Poetry has a consciousness of its own and belongs to everyone. Every poem we ever read will meet us and touch us all differently. The commentaries share the context and the questions that gave birth to the words of each poem. Far from an attempt at an answer, these poems and their commentaries give rise to reflections that may shine the light onto yet another question.

A journey of any kind is never linear. A journey is more circular, maybe even spiral. The poems in this book follow no chronological order. Harry Chapin sang it best "No straight lines make up my life; And all my roads have bends; There's no clear-cut beginnings; And so far, no dead-ends." Life will always be a dance between ego and soul, love, and fear. Our life is a circle. Our life is a never-ending poem.

Awakening. The poems in this section reflect the opening of my real eyes, my soul eyes, as I was gazing upon that second mountain! The voice of my soul was finally getting through the noise as I started to have the deeper conversations of life, including the one with my "self". Love and light were starting to penetrate through the layers of armour and through all of the veils that I had collected on the conquering climb up the first mountain. Realizations came as egoic lessons as I looked back to look ahead, to be present. Poetry was penetrating my defenses. Life begins on the other side of fear.

Head to Heart- These poems reflect the bright sadness of falling upwards. This sadness of reacting slowly being replaced by creativity, imagination, compassion, humor, intuition, joy, bliss, and love as I learned how to climb the ladder of selves by slowly removing the layers that had weighed upon me like a knight in rusty armour. The arrival of self love led to forgiveness and awareness of the present moment in that space between breaths and heartbeats. My heart was opening up to the light of love as it entered my body to melt away fear. I was developing gratitude for my ego as I heard the voice of my soul calling my name. I am love.

Heart to Soul- These poems follow the path as I travelled from me to we only to arrive where I had started and knowing this place for the first time as a new, cherished gift. I was choosing to see through the eyes of love every single day. We always have been enough. Whole. A body in a soul, on a collision with Grace. Light and love were flowing to me, through me and from me. A circle. A soul circle. Transcending the self, I felt connected with everything. Acceptance and forgiveness were leading to healing. We are love.

This book is an invitation to your own soul journey of purpose and exploration as you live your own beautiful questions. The answers to our most intense questions are not how to guides. They are poetry. The path of discovery is to find and to be found by the poetry within. Our very life is a poem in itself. The very door to our soul opens from the inside.

As French Philosopher Pierre Teilhard de Chardin professed, "We are spiritual beings having a human experience."

Have you been to yourself?
In all of this noise
Are you living your dreams?
Does your soul have a voice?
When you close your eyes,
what do you see?
Where your heart meets your soul,
who must you be?
Will your why be your way?
How will you tell your story?

May poetry find you as a prayer. May her words see you, hear you, validate you, hold you, soothe you, free you, forgive you and heal you. May her words bless you. May poetry guide you to the windows and doors of spacious, sacred, and deeper possibilities. As Grace announces the harvest of her presence, may the flower of your life unfold all around you.

May this book be a companion on your exploration to purpose. Heart broken loose on the wind, soul ignited, awakening to love. Awakening to you. May you fall upwards on your journey. Home

May you always be Cuoreous!

Thank you to all of the poets mentioned in this book and beyond whose words have inspired me. Thank you to my friends, to my guides, and to my family for creating poetry with me every day on this mysterious and beautiful journey.

♡
Awakening

Morning Ritual

I awoke today
To the quiet darkness
Whispering my name
A warm ache greeting me
Like a child on Christmas morning
Calling me
To rise up
Telling me
A new day is arriving
Reminding me
That love is a choice
A choice that I create
Every fucking day
I tenderly sip a fresh cup of coffee
That dances on my lips
Romances my nostrils
I greet this new day
As a cherished gift
Thankful in gratitude
I am so alive
I sit and bless her
And as
Grace
Announces the harvest
Of her presence
The flower of my life
Unfolds around me

Morning Ritual

Written in the early morning darkness in mid October 2020, in London. Rumi taught us "The breeze at dawn has secrets to tell you. Don't go back to sleep." There is magic at this altar of dawn. The loyalty of light breaks through the darkness. The sacred gift of Grace is unfolding all around me. The present. Silence. Solitude. Stillness. The kiss of fresh coffee holding hands with possibility. A child on Christmas morning! A new day. A new dawn. Feeling good. A ritual.

Essence to Crux

She haunts me
The daughter of time
Mystery swathed in
layers of possibility
I slowly undress her
as she sings to my heart
We speak our own language
Words are not necessary
She is a cavernous ache
Persistently growing
The absence of all fear
As wisdom
She knows I am nothing
As love
She knows I am everything
I am a poem she writes
as I dance between the two
I crave her
She is the presence
of enduring longing
Essence to crux
She is truth
Hand in hand I walk
with her
into the unknown
The only path home

Essence to Crux

Written the day after Morning Ritual in mid October 2020, in London. Truth is the daughter of time as Sir Francis Bacon wrote five hundred years ago. Our life itself is a poem as time weds us to our own story. We are all awakening to our own true essence on a journey to crux. Mystery swathed in layers of possibility. David Whyte eloquently writes in his poem The Journey, "Someone has written something new in the ashes of your life. You are not leaving. Even as the light fades quickly now, you are arriving."

The second mountain appears, and we fall upwards. In our own disappearance our truth will set us free.

Confusion

I can still vividly remember
the brand new
Shiny box of crayons
The smell of wax and possibility
My first day of school
Red, yellow, and orange
Blue, purple and green
All giving way
to the king and queen
Black and white
The invitation
to show our best result
I decorated the naked picture
with the joyous dancing colours
of my singing heArt
My excited body trembling
as the pastels spoke through me
Possessing my own hand
in a mesmerizing baptism with
the sweet flowing river of creativity
What I now know was love
stared back at my eyes
A consecration of connection
The gift of innocence
lost that day in a cruel lie
Their displeasure cloaking me
in a heavy new disguise
that only now I have come to realize
The magical intention of life
was to never stay within the lines

Confusion

Written in February 2022, in London, as part of the incredible poet Tanya Markul's writing course in support of creating this book of poetry. I was asked to write about a time when I was sharing a gift that I had created as a child, and something then happened that I did not expect; the title of this poem reflecting the name of that emotion. I was five and my first memory of school was to colour a picture. We were given a brand-new box of crayons! The Crayola pack of eight. I can still smell and taste the waxy magic to this day. I left my heart on the page. To my surprise, I was scolded, told I was sloppy and taught to stay between the lines. Life is so much more interesting out beyond those lines! We create a bigger picture! We create a bigger life!

Curtain Call

We all know the place
That same old worn out stage
seductively so familiar
Where the pleasing of performance
has slowly become our cage
Projecting from the limelight
on that raised
pedestal of belonging
Where we will go barefoot
to sell the kiss in a scene
And as the applause
comes right on cue
In the shallow laughter
of pretending
You know
that you never really knew
How to play
the part
of you

Curtain Call

Written in late January 2022, in London in a state of reflection.

We all want acceptance and validation in our lives. We all want to be seen. It is tempting to continue to behave in favour of approval; acting, entertaining, and pleasing from a script that we ourselves never wrote. We will all start there. Remaining on that old familiar stage may not allow us to truly discover our real innate self. Imitation is not the sincerest form of flattery, listening is. It starts with hearing our own deep voice first, being brave and vulnerable to follow our heart and intuition. We are already enough. Our souls already know the way. Our way. We all want to sing our own songs and to share our own words with the world before we take that final curtain call. To create is to courageously bring something into existence that isn't there already, to make its way into sacred expression in the world. Our real self. Believing is seeing! Wisdom is the journey from imitation to creation.

Voice

You were
Taken from me
A long time ago
I learned to hide from you
When you tried
To find me
Once again
I turned away
Running scared
I did not recognize you
You were a stranger
You were always there
You were so quiet
I could not hear you
You did carry me
Away from danger
When I heard
Your loud screams
My screams
As the chaos
Became quieter
You called to me
Nurtured me
Nourished me
I felt the warm embrace
Of myself letting go
Surrendering in stillness
In sweet solitude
I started to hear you
In moments
When my mind
Was quiet
When my heart was full
You greeted me warmly

With deep tenderness
You came to visit
More often
I learned to listen
With you
We became friends
I learned to trust you
You grew on me
I started to love you
To dance with you
You brought me alive
I was seen through you
I was heard through you
You taught me I could sing
My own song
Loudly
Accepted
You have set me free
I cherish you
My beautiful voice
You are my soul

Voice

Written in May 2020, in London as the weight of the covid pandemic met me with a job layoff and orders to stay home. I was out of work for the first time in thirty years. With quiet time to read and write, that deep voice, my voice, got louder! I had not written much, if at all since 2016. In that silence and solitude, I felt my heart opening. Rumi said "Sit quietly and listen for a voice that will say, be more silent. As that happens your soul starts to revive". I heard my soul singing to me. Intuition. Interoception. Learning to recognize and trust our own voice is a soul journey unto itself. To be brave and courageous to sing our own song is feeling the rapture of being alive! The second mountain had come for me. Poetry had found me once again. Through the cracks, the light was getting inside of me. Love is a language that needs no words.

Red Barn

I drove away from the rising sun
A red barn
stood far up on the horizon
Mysteriously beautiful
in a sea of harvested tranquility
It beckoned to me
Captivating my eyes
Burning my soul
I could not look away
It called to me like a siren
Yesterday
was a reflection
in the rear view mirror
I met the big sky today
She took my hand
and met my heart
Wrapped herself around me
All I could see in every direction
Was forever

Red Barn

Written on November 5, 2020, travelling across the prairies. I was helping a good friend move west from London to Edmonton. This was my first ever experience meeting the big sky. I scribbled down the final version from my head that evening in a hotel in Saskatoon, the Paris of the prairies, as the US election played out in the background. The flattened illusion of distance in space dancing with the beauty of Grace. I felt swallowed by the horizon. I left my "body" while on that drive. A feeling of forever wrapping me in a blanket of connection with everything.

Fitting In

The unquenchable quest for acceptance
The winding road
I have always travelled
The layers of beliefs
dressed upon me
in the well intentioned
prayers of fear
The words themselves
Spells
that magically appear

        Attracting
        the very encounter
        the invocation
        was uttered to shelter
        The undesired thought
        the leading role
        in a production
        never rehearsed
        Yet the lines and the songs
        are known by heart
        My Queen
        this need to be seen
        a heavy cross that I bear
        crawling along this track
        One step forward
        Two steps back

Fitting In

Written in March 2022, in London. Looking back at old patterns. The need to be accepted speaks loudly to me. I was reading Abraham Hicks', "The Vortex", at the time and I finally understood how focussing on what we don't want to happen can manifest that very undesired event itself to come into our existence. We will never leave a footprint if we are tiptoeing through life. Acceptance comes from the inside not the outside. As Robert Holden says, "No amount of self improvement can make up for lack of self acceptance." Life is a journey. Our journey. Sometimes it is one step forward, two steps back. We are all just dancing in the dark. Trust the dance steps!

Letting Grow

Grasping too hard
in the shadows of control
The fear of loss
never letting this ship
leave the sheltered harbour
Anchored in the storm
without learning how to ride
the waves or the shifting tide
The only way to walk
is to fall down trying
In the flailing frenzy
of staying above
the chaos of the
current of change
Sometimes letting go
is the only way to grow

Letting Grow

Written in early February 2022, in London. Life is a swimming lesson, letting go and learning to keep our head above the water to breathe. Learning to ride out the waves is a practice. Change is inevitable. Growth is optional. Rumi shared, "Life is a balance of holding on and letting go". Let our past be our compass, never an anchor. Claudia Black wisely said, "Forgiving is not forgetting. It is remembering and letting go." Half of our life is hidden from us and exists beyond our control, in the cloaked embrace of mystery. Life blossoms on the other side of fear. Letting go to grow. Falling upwards.

Time

I have always been
bound to her
She is my lover
Perpetually present
Yet fleeting
like the wind
All ways
the wisest counsellor
She is the Queen
of my existence
The ghost
of all experiences
Creator of all things
yet to come
She gives me
what she will
Not always what I desire
She is the kiss
of a moment
The hands on the clock
I plead with her
to caress me slowly
as she sweetly sings me
to my grave

Time

Written in late October 2020. Pericles professes, "Time is the wisest counsellor." Time is our perpetual lover, and the queen of all thieves. She is our constant companion.

With her we spend our lives
Although we are not buying
For she is free
Nonetheless
never to be possessed
Once she leaves
she cannot come back
All the same she remains
forever present
To give of her
is the most precious of gifts
Yet she is the greatest of thieves
Not for a moment to be caught
Looking forwards we illusively try
to overtake her
Continuously looking backwards
to remember her
She stares back from the mirror
Our wrinkles quietly whispering her name

I Don't Know

I have no expectations of you
You only ever need to be
Who you are
I do not bring
Wisdom
or answers
I am not my past
All we have is
This moment
This place
This frontier
This intersection
Between
Who we were
Who we will be
Embracing all we are
Now
We hold this space
With us
For us
This most beautiful truth
Intimacy
We sit together
in this precious space
Presence
Living as one
Together
Here in
I don't know

I Don't Know

Written in late January 2021, in London.

The Covid pandemic was 10 months old, and uncertainty ruled the day. I was finding the courage to say, "I don't know". I was living the questions. I was learning to hold space for myself and for others. We were all collectively living in a shared liminal space, embracing the intimate mystery of the unknown. The only certainty is uncertainty. The real conversation of life is always in the here and the now. Anne Lamott shares that "The mystery of grace will meet us where we are, but she will never leave us where she found us."

Aurora

In that fleeting moment
where the darkness
surrenders her light
That sacred threshold
where the coming day
embraces the release
of the waning night
The lessons of yesterday
caressing the possibility
of the moment
The ghosts of the past
only beads on the necklace
of time
The angel of dawn
brings her gift
of forgiveness
And you realize
in the healing blue hue
of truth
The only thing
stopping you from
arriving
is leaving

Aurora

Written in early December 2021. Aurora is the Roman goddess of dawn. The queen of light. There is magic in that predawn blue hue of truth as Aurora prepares to wrap us in the colourful gift of a new day. A promise of invitation and possibility. Yesterday has already let us go. Her lessons bestowed upon us. Yesterday is history. Tomorrow is a mystery. Today is a gift. The present. Presence. Often the only thing stopping us from arriving is leaving.

HEAD TO HEART

Through the Eyes of Love

Awakening in the darkness of a new day
Dwelling in that sacred space
between a dream and a body
The prayer of breath
Greeting the ascension of time
In the fleeting moment
before judgement arrives
I choose to see
through the eyes
of love

Through the Eyes of Love

Written in early November 2021, in London.

We start each day in that dimension between body and soul and in that space between dream and awake. Our first seventeen seconds of awareness sets the intention for the day. In that moment before judgement arrives, we can choose to see through the eyes of love. Flow in love. Stay there. Believing is seeing. Another morning ritual. As Rumi reminds us, "Love is the bridge between you and everything".

Coffee

A taste of a new day
Wet and warm
on my curious lips
Yesterday is gone
Tomorrow is just a thought
never a guarantee
The aroma of the present
fills this time of space
Waking my sleeping heart
as I meet myself again
A spirit
Surrendering
on a journey
to devotion

Coffee

Written in early January 2022, in London. Coffee is an elixir! I am called to wake in the dark before dawn. My sacred time. Solitude. Silence. Stillness. Coffee is my constant morning companion that I share with the rising sun. Combined with the harvest of Grace I am amazed at the clarity of the thoughts that flow through me at this time. These two hours are a ritual. With cup in hand, I celebrate the new day. I sniff the invitation. The aroma kisses my face. My lips explode as I take that first sip. The swirling liquid saturating my very soul with warmth and possibility. My body stimulated to action. My heart is open and energized as my blood dances to the magic of the moment. Coffee is a meditation. The flower of my life unfolds around me. The words find me and with a pen in hand I slowly turn coffee into ink.

I Am Just a Man

I frown and I smile
I laugh and I cry
There is love in my heart
And wonder in my eyes
I have witnessed new birth
I have beheld death
I have felt blissful joy
I have struggled for breath
I have been a father
I have loved a wife
I wake up every morning
Do the best that I can
Live each day I am given
I am just a man
I am a man
I am just a man
I have felt strong love
And the pain from loss
Cried from sheer happiness
Carried my own cross
I wander this world
But I am not lost
I have collected moments
Not things of great cost
I have basked in the sun
I have been soaked by the rain
My dreams have been broken
I have raised them again
I can be a fool
Righteous as a plan
I count all of my blessings
I am just a man
I am a man
I am just a man

I Am Just a Man

Written in Skerries, Ireland in mid July 2016. After the enchanting enlightenment fueled mystery of wonder in the highlands of Scotland, the emerald island met me with a deep calm spirit of awe. I wrote this poem in minutes on a morning walk along the beach. Looking outward at the horizon but starting to look inward to myself. I felt a sense of gratitude for a life well lived and the calling of spiritual growth still yet to come. Shakespeare's words were resonating, "The meaning in life is to find your gift. The purpose in life is to give it away." I was starting to feel the connection to something much bigger than myself. The light of love was starting to find the cracks in my heart!

Forgotten Not Lost

The heavy crescendo
of compromise
Loudly camouflages
The sweet tender song
of truth
Can you still hear your own voice
calling to you?
The wind
has changed direction
You numbly sway
to the masquerade of succumbing
Abandoning your passion
for the peaceful truce
of comfortable convenience
You learn to drown
in the familiar tears
of expectation
The earth
still moves underneath your feet
Yet you are
Standing still
Obediently sinking
into the languishing sands
of your own
Disappearance

Forgotten Not Lost

Written over Christmas Eve 2020, in London. I was looking back to look ahead. Christmas is magical as a winter soulstice yields to the long quiet darkness of contemplation as it meets the scheduled demands of a busy holiday. An emotional dance of contrast. This poem is a reflection upon awakening at the top of the first mountain. I was looking in the mirror and not recognizing my "self". My own eyes were camouflaged. I was an egoic knight disguised in heavy rusty armour. The weight of a lifetime of expectations were drowning out the song of my deeper voice in the echoes of compromise.

The First Step Home

Like a universal wound
The ache of home
never leaves you
In the stillness
between your thoughts
You hear your own soul
softly singing
from the depths
of forgotten essence
A faint whisper of Grace
resonating to the very beat
of your own heart
You begin to breathe
into the creative rhythm
of surrender
A radiant star shines
on the distant horizon
announcing a new birth
An awakening
As your feet
find the solid ground
of your own truth
You take the only step
that you can make
The one toward
Yourself

The First Step Home

Written on December 26, 2020, in London rewriting the Christmas story as my own. Our own. We all share the same wound of forgotten love. We are the star on the horizon. This poem sings of a rebirth via a journey inside, coming home to love. We are already enough, gazing out at the second mountain as the mist starts to clear. I heard my own true voice still a whisper yet rising above the noise. My heart was opening to its song. My song. The world's song. A love song. We were always the gift. Our soul is the package we unwrap underneath all the layers of conditioning. Love has always been the present. Love lives in the moment. Here and now. A child on Christmas morning!

The first step I must take is the one towards my "self". I surrender to love. I let go and fall "upwards".

The Spring Moon

The equinox
was calling to my bones
The pull of energy
The madness of lunacy
A tidal fever
of forgiveness
Beckoning for change
The light now reaching
deeper
farther into the
darkness
Uncovering the dusty corners
of the shadows
where the hurt is hidden
beyond the reach
of healing
Self love
still only a crescent
too blind
to be fully embraced
The shame still
hiding the gratitude
The guilt remained
In this moment of
awakening
now touched by
the illumination of
the whole of the
Moon
I found what I had
forgotten
now there for me
to clearly see
I broke off the chains
Opened up the old box
and I set myself
Free

The Spring Moon

Written at the spring equinox as it collided with a full moon in March 2022, in London. The energy of the full moon super fueled by the spirit of an equinox created a poetic fever. The words boiled over. Mark Twain said, "Everyone is a moon, and has a dark side which he never shows to anybody." This poem echoes Mike Scott of the Waterboys singing with Carl Jung as the shadows of old repressed events get illuminated by the whole of the moon. "I love you" is the ringing chorus sung by the angel of forgiveness. We need to look into the mirror everyday and sing this back to ourselves. Life loves us. Self love is always the first step to forgiveness and healing.

Unwynd

For years we can't see clearly
The clock rules our life
In the throws of parenthood
Being husband or wife
We put in our time at work
We trade our hours for pay
Our kids grow up so quickly
And there comes a day
We look into the mirror
We can't believe our age
Every minute has been worth it
But time has turned a page
We all search for meaning
Our purpose to find
When it is our thme
The knot will unwynd
We still have desires
There is more we need to be
We feel an ache in our gut
It wakes us from our sleep
It is not about more money
Nor a need to be right
We want to give love
We want to shine light
Our spirit cries for growth
Beyond where we have been
Our soul longs for insight
Beyond what we have seen
We all search for meaning
Our purpose to find
When it is our thme
The knot will unwynd
The world is full of signs
and synchronicities

Once we open up our hearts
It is there for us to see
It is not enlightenment
Or wisdom per se
A fervid sense of being
Will arrive one day
The way lies before us
For all that we can be
We are the creators
Of our own destiny
We all search for meaning
Our purpose to find
When it is our thme
The knot will unwynd

Unwynd

Written in Kirkwall, Orkney Islands, Scotland in July 2016. On the winding drive north from Glasgow we stopped in Fort William to stretch our legs. In a souvenir shop I saw a Celtic necklace that had a story with it discussing the "Destiny Knot". This legend stuck with me, Scots spelling, and all. The magical mystique of Orkney with her standing stones and megalithic history thousands of years old opened a portal to another dimension. The words came to call, and this poem was born in a late-night frenzy under a midnight Scottish sun. "Fate will unwind as it must", asserts poet Buron Raffel. My heart was speaking. Destiny was calling.

Stone

I took a block of
rough stone
I asked myself
What do I need?
As my hammer
cracked open
the heart of the rock
I asked myself
What do I want?
As my chisel worked
the debris
I asked myself
What do I desire?
I saw the angel
 in the marble
and I carved
until I set myself
free

Stone

Written in November 2021, in London. This poem is a shout out to Michelangelo who, "saw the angel in the marble and set her free". Our soul already knows who we are underneath all this rusty armour and inside of this hardened hunk of stone that we have slowly become. As we sculpt our own lives, we are the carver that will unleash our own hidden beauty. We are also a unique wellspring of provenanced being waiting to be set free. Love is the chisel.

Real Eyes

A perpetual seeker, my quest was the cause
A wayfarer on a journey to enlightenment
Climbing this second mountain of life
To gaze upon the fiery face of truth
Standing at the edge of a cliff
With no where left to roam
The calm winds from the horizon of awareness
Caressing the bone deep ache for home
My heart cracking open to an awakening
The questions are the answers
The very presence of being
That patiently pumps through my veins
My bare feet meeting the solid ground of my own soul
Surrendering to real eyes
I take the only step I can ever truly make
The one that goes inside

Real Eyes

Written late February 2022, in London in reflection. "Real Eyes", is a homophone for "realize". Two words having the same pronunciation but different meanings. While pondering the possible images for the cover of this book, I was drawn to a picture with me standing at the edge of a cliff gazing out at the horizon in July 2020. It was a very symbolic picture. I was perpetually searching and seeking from the outside for direction. At that time my heart was cracking open, and I started to look inwards with a new lens. Antione de Saint-Exupery said it so wisely, "It is only with the heart that one can see rightly; what is essential is invisible to the eye." Cuoreosity. The heArt of Being. Living the questions. A soul's journey that has always been a pilgrimage back to my "self". A circle. A soul circle. Coming home to love. A "real eyes-ation" that the only step I could ever truly make was the one towards my "self"

Freedom

Where does freedom really lie?
Freedom is never a script
At no time a judge
Not a condition to meet
It is not there
To discover
It already exists
Not outside
Deep Inside
In the surrender
To the here
To the now
Being
In the moment
Letting go
Head to heart
Trusting boundaries
Void of expectations
Full of compassion
For who I am
Of why I am
For who we are
From me to we
Us

Freedom

Written in mid February 2021, in London. What is freedom? Reflecting on that time, I was poetically detailing my journey from head to heart. My heart was opening as I was travelling on a road from thought to expression. I was learning to let go of judgement and the expectation, both from myself and others. I was learning to embrace vulnerability, self acceptance, and self love on a journey to presence, clarity, and surrender. Choosing love is never a linear process. It represents more of a circle. A soul circle! Choosing love is a daily practice. Who am I? I am love. We are love. We are already whole. We are not broken. Believing is seeing! Freedom is seeing through the eyes of love. Freedom lies on the other side of fear.

Born Again

Reaching for the light
You break free
Any barriers
Defenceless
Against the strength
Of the essence
That drives all desire
Wings unfolding
As they meet the invitation
Of life
Kissing the freedom
Of air
Your purpose
Already known
As you open your eyes
Fighting for breath
Startled by the cries
Of your own
Arrival

Born Again

Written in late April 2022, in London.

This poem depicts our soul's journey as it crosses the threshold into this vessel of life. We astonishingly arrive as we abruptly awaken into this body. Our sacred expression is already burning as the very being of our spirit. We are born again into this experience. The hand of our divine purpose is guiding us toward the light of love. We are born again into living these questions. If life is a maze, we can get lost trying to find our way out. However, inside a labyrinth we will find our own centre. A soul journey. The very lessons of life dance with our essence as we explore this spiral labyrinth of sweet mysterious existence to come home to love.

HEART TO SOUL

Original Artwork
Kelly McKay Millard

Dawn

I awoke today
A stranger
At this threshold
where the magic of dreams
caress the soft whispers
of a new day
My heart dancing
to the invitation
of new beginnings
Anticipation
singing to me
I lie warm and snug
embraced by this gift
Breathing
Held closely
and kissed on my cheeks
by my wings
Being and Believing
I rise slowly
Grateful
Opening the door
to myself
I step across
the verge
and fall in love
all over again

Dawn

Written June 12, 2021, on a morning walk in the forest behind my house in London. A familiar theme, the gratitude of waking to a new day. We are always on a journey from darkness to light. A circle of belonging. Dawn is a time of possibility and promise. As John O Donohue shares in Anam Cara, "Dawn is the ultimate surprise. When love awakens in your life, in the night of your heart it is like the dawn breaking within you." When love awakens in your life, it is like a rebirth, a new beginning. Dawn. We meet ourselves as a stranger and fall in love with ourselves all over again. A morning ritual. A new beginning.

The Winter Rain

In the calling
winds of change
My spirit wanders
somewhere
between a body
and a soul
Learning the lessons
of letting go
Like water
caught halfway
between sleet
and snow
Tears on my face
freezing to pain
as I meet
the winter rain

The Winter Rain

Written in late November 2021, in London walking in a hard driving sleet, half rain and half snow. Winter was arriving. Change was in the air. We are always meeting the world in a state of change, between spaces, between seasons and between dimensions. Water is our mirror. She takes on the shape of her container. Us. Head or heart. Love or fear. Body or soul. Water is always deeper than our own reflection. Author Masaru Emoto beautifully shares, "Water is the mirror that has the ability to show us what we cannot see."

Dusk

I sit back
An old friend
to the light
At this approach
Where the wisdom
of darkness
gently calls back
Her colours
My soul awakened
to the reaching hand
of Grace
Summoning me
to the oracle
of dreams
My spirit
Resonating
to the sweet touch
of truth
Softly kissing my lips
as my eyes
slowly close
Greeting her
and dancing
to the music
of a little death
Only to be
Reborn
A stranger
Welcomed to the gift
once again

Dusk

Written June 12, 2021, in London as a follow up to Dusk. Dawn to dusk. Light to darkness. A celebration of another day. The gift. Bookending gratitude at dawn and dusk is another daily ritual. How we end our day sets up how we begin our day. Our evening ritual may just be a morning ritual as well. We are not scared of the dark. We are scared of what is inside of it. Scientists tell us that black is the absence of light. Artists tell us that black is the presence of all colours. Colour is descriptive. Black and white is interpretive. Poetry is black ink on white paper painting pictures with words. Quoting Francis Bacon "In order for the light to shine so brightly, darkness must be present." Poetry allows the darkness to become conscious. Present. If darkness is the absence of light, then ego is the absence of awareness. Without self reflection there is blindness in darkness. Shadows owe their birth to light. As Rumi reveals "If everything around seems dark, look again, you may be the light."

The Wheels of Change

As the wheels
of change
Start to roll
faster
And the ghosts
of doubt
arrive to be
fed
Will you run
and make them
your master
Will you leave
your dreams
for dead
Will you
be authentic
and live
in your heart
Or will you
dance with
the what ifs
in your head
Will you stand
beside me
Graced in faith
as love takes a deep hold
Will you be brave
Trusting
that in letting go
that we will
never be alone
Knowing in this
sweet surrender
We have all
come to
walk each other
Home

The Wheels of Change

Written in mid May 2021, in London. This poem is a conversation between ego and soul living the questions! Life happens on the other side of fear. The ego is a lousy master but a wonderful servant. Coming home to love is our destiny and the geography of our soul. As Carl Jung said, "The first half of life is developing a healthy ego, the second half is going inward and letting it go". Ram Dass elaborating that the ego is about separation and the soul is about love. "Souls love. That's what souls do. Egos don't, but souls do. Become a soul, look around, and you'll be amazed-all the beings around you are souls. Be one, see one. When many people have this heart connection, then we will know that we are all one, we human beings all over the planet. We will be one. One love. And don't leave out the animals, and trees, and clouds, and galaxies-it's all one. It's one energy."

This echoes David Brooks "The Second Mountain". If the first mountain is the safety of our ego, the second is the song of our soul. Individual to interdependence. The transcendence of self. As Sharon Blackie illiterates, "Its not about slaying the dragon, but about harnessing his special skills and making him part of the team". One love. Connection. Grace. Faith. A soul journey.

I will give Ram Dass the final word, "We are all just walking each other home"!

Letting Go

Broken wide open
Raw
My feet slipping
down the rungs
of this ladder
My arms desperately
clinging
My hands gripping
squeezing
I can't hold on
any longer
My breath is gone
as I fall
My heart
whispers
to my tears
Surrender
Letting go
has always been
the only truth
From a fetal position
I rise up
Tall
I take the first small
step
Grounded
My spirit smiling
as my soul
carries
me
Home

Letting Go

Written in early February 2021, in London. Almost one year into the Covid pandemic. I was holding on tightly to a world that was changing. Surrendering to the change is a practice! I was letting go of this need to control. The well known "Serenity Prayer", echoes within this poem. Mindfulness is being present in the moment. The journey from head to heart is a daily practice. A prayer. A blessing. A ritual. A choice. A poem. Letting go is embracing the unknown. Thich Nhat Hanh professed that "Letting go gives us freedom."

Eye of the Storm

Have you ever been struck
by lightening?
Your heart seen?
Your essence heard?
Your body dancing to the songs
that saved you on your journey through
Your mind numb with drunken candor
celebrating your truth
Your soul knows who you must become
This path gloriously unfolding all around you
A blossoming flower
The stranger you now see in the mirror
is the lover
who has brought you home
Untethered and naked
You have arrived
in the eye of your storm

Eye of the Storm

Written in late November 2020, in London. This was written as a reflection on the journey to healing. Life is a storm and at the centre of the spiralling labyrinth we will find ourself. The eye of our storm is that calm awareness and clarity of our soul. Louise Hay describes this journey so well in her book "Life Loves You". It starts with self awareness and self acceptance on a path to self love. Forgiveness is an act of self love. Forgiveness is letting go. Forgiveness leads to healing. Healing is a release of the chains of our past. Our life does not move on if we have not moved on and stripped off all the layers we collected on the way. We will then be able to see love looking back at us in the mirror. If we do not forgive, we keep giving our future to the past and we are not living in the present. We can't change our past, but we can change the story we give to it. Robert Holden illuminates it best "The door to our soul opens from the inside", "Our soul waits for us. Our ego must be willing to let the light in! Our ego has to open the door"! My soul was waiting. My ego was ready. The door was covered in weeds and rusted shut. It took a few pulls, but it opened into a beautiful garden. Into that garden I go every day to lose my mind and feed my soul. Love held the key. Love is always the way. Home.

Destiny

Have I been to myself?
In all of this noise
Am I living my truth?
Can I hear my own voice?
When I close my eyes
Who do I see?
Where my heart meets my soul
Who must I be?
This invisible force
Pulling me towards
Who I am
Why I am
Why I am here
This call of Grace
This taste
of deeper meaning
This song
of collective purpose
The harvest of my life
Feeding me
to the angel
of my destiny
Holding her hand
as she softly
sings me
Home

Destiny

Written in late February 2021 in London. Destiny! The queen of the grand old questions that like faint echoes ferment into a powerful presence. Author Steven Pressfield called it the invisible hand. He says that we are all put here for a reason. That destiny lives inside of us. It has been there from birth, and maybe before that. We can't see it, touch it, we can't measure it. But we can feel it. John O'Donohue says, "Your soul knows the geography of your destiny." "All the possibilities of your human destiny are asleep in your soul. You are here to realize and honour these possibilities. When love comes into your life, unrecognized dimensions of your destiny awaken and blossom and grow. Possibility is the secret heart of time." The pull of our very soul is always guiding us towards our purpose from the cradle to the grave. Rabbi Harold Kushner pronounced, "We nourish our soul by fulfilling our destiny."

Limitless

Who have I become?
I am a stranger
yet I am how
I have always been
What is my name?
I have lived a thousand lives
I have been called many things
in tongues
I cannot remember
My heart
ever a translator
For now I can see
that I found the way
Home
Across a threshold
few can ever know
Why do I then shake?
Filled with a strange energy
These tears of becoming
they must now flow
as I let go
of who I was
I am love
Daring to live
in heaven and on earth
Tasting sweet
Surrender
Learning to fly
Wings
Take me to a garden
where the souls of my own
Bless me
and hold me
Wrapped in a blanket

that glows with my tears
Setting me free
to become this perpetual
stranger
Breathing in the moments
Stretching beyond
the boundaries
that contain my body
I am a soul
Limitless
Breathing in
possibility
Knowing
that I have never left
I have only just
Arrived

Limitless

Written in late July 2020, in London. Breathing into possibility and filled with a deeper awareness. The heart has its own language. We are never leaving, only arriving. Rumi wisely sharing, "The soul is a stranger trying to find a home, somewhere that is not a where." "If light is in your heart. You will find your way home." We are already home. Head to heart. Heart to soul. The door only opens from the inside. "Maybe you are searching in the branches for what only appears in the roots".

Threshold

In the heart of darkness
lives invisible light
That dawn breaks into colour
held possible by the night
It is so strange to be here
This mystery remains persistent
at the threshold of all knowing
and unconscious bewilderment
Where imagination takes a curved path
avoiding the well trodden way straight
to journey inwards through a forgotten gate
where our spirit waits with benevolent humility
for our homecoming to this seat of Grace
Where time is the mother of existence
Where destiny is sculpted by our soul
That space where identity is fermenting
harmonizing from a self into a whole
There are no maps to this spiritual domain
but the way is peculiarly familiar
We have travelled to a place
that we have previously known
We have crossed over the threshold
only to return back home
To that sanctuary where we have never been wounded
The altar of confidence and tranquility
Where potential resides in endless possibility
We emerge with the recognition of true being
Full presence in the clarity of awareness
Embraced and nourished by a deep fulfilling love
Realization becomes actualization
where information engenders transformation
Outside the waves will always ebb and flow
As the ocean we will just watch them come and go
Connected to the rhythm of the universe

whirling and dancing at one with the source
The gift of the moment never presumed
At the end of the day
comes the darkness of night
Once dusk takes back her colour
We will still embrace the light

Threshold

Written in late July 2020, in London. A soul friend had sent me a copy of John O'Donohue's beautiful book Anam Cara. This book cracked my essence wide open. We are a body in a soul! A threshold suddenly opened in front of me. This door only opened towards me. I stepped "inwards" to meet my authentic "self". Everything made sense in a sweet kiss of revelation. I felt like I had been in this space before. I felt swallowed whole by the presence of Grace.

This awareness echoing what TS Eliot famously wrote in "Little Gidding", the final section of the astounding "Four Quartets". "We shall not cease from exploration and the end of all our exploring will be to arrive where we started and know the place for the first time." Presence. Being. Transcendence of the self as part of something beyond. Connected to Grace. We are souls having a human experience. As CS Lewis confessed "You do not have a soul. You are a soul. You have a body." A body in a soul!

The words came quickly as a rhyme. The poem speaks to the gift of the day. Dawn to dusk. Light and dark. All colour is still present in darkness. The light we see is our own reflected back to us by source herself. We are the light! The invisible in our shadows becoming visible. We are all pilgrims on the same quest to clarity. The poem speaks to the circularity of our soul journey. It may take lifetimes to become awareness. We are not lost. We are transforming and transcending. As Meister Eckhart exclaims "We all are returning back to a place in our soul that has never been wounded". We are all coming home to love.

Collision With Grace

Once in your lifetime
She happens to you
Time suddenly disrobes
Slips her dress off
Consecrates all belonging
Angelic waves swallow your body
To meet your soul
Staring deeply into her eyes
The sweet aching arrival of home
Naked truth kissing your face
As you are baptized
In a collision
with Grace

Collision With Grace

Written in early December 2020, in London. Life is often akin to living on a clock pendulum that swings between the guilt of the past and the fear of the future. In all of that movement it is never easy to find the present. It is hard to be in the moment of the here and now let alone to stay there. This is my best go at putting words to that rare feeling of being swallowed whole by the universe. The magical moment where we become one with "everything". The soul is that dimension of awareness beyond the limits or destiny of the body. That space where even time herself does not exist. Transcendence. A collision with Grace!

Who Am I?

I am meaning
I am being
I witness thoughts
And let them go
I am the moment
Freedom
Possibility
Are all that I know
I own nothing
Embrace all change
I just keep breathing
Generate the space
I am joy
I am peace
Pure consciousness
Gratitude and Grace
Mindful oneness
True life force
I am creative
Resourceful and whole
Universal mind
I am the source
Spiritual energy
An all loving soul
I am limitless
I have all I need
I am enough
Expectation free
Non judgemental
Nothing to find
I am selfless
Infinitely divine
I am transcendence
Wisdom hereof

I am here and now
Unconditional love
You ask me who I am?
For I am you
I am you

Who Am I?

Written in mid June 2020, in London. Purpose and exploration in the presence of wonder. Source. Grace. The universe. Non duality intersecting with Syd Bank's Three Principles dancing with transcendence herself. Awareness. Consciousness. Universal mind. Thought. Being. We are unconditional love. Connection. Oneness. We are all here to show each other God. Who am I? A soul having a human experience. Who am I? I am you! Rumi declaring all existence is part of the same source, "All souls are one".

♡ Epilogue

A Blessing for Cuoreosity

As the flower of grace
blossoms to find you
may you live life true to yourself
shedding what is false
to be who you are here to be.
May you be courageous and brave
allowing your heart
to be cracked wide open
in a deep embrace
with the intimacy of vulnerability.
May you let go of judgement
for believing is truly seeing.
Listening is the sincerest form of respect.
May the gate of empathy
always lead you into the arms of compassion.
Self love is always the first step
on the path to forgiveness and healing.
The only gift we can truly give to another
is the fruit of the harvest
of our own authenticity.
May you accept the invitation
of the deeper conversations
that will shape your spirit
as you live into the light
of the very questions themselves.
The pilgrimage to the inside
 is where we will find ourselves
 at the centre of the labyrinth.
May you look inwards
before you go outside
to seek your answers.
Introspection is our truest adventure
as doing flows from being.
We are human beings.

In the unique rediscovery of your own purpose
may the intention of your sacred expression
make its way into the world.
Our soul knows the geography of our destiny.
We are souls having a human experience.
In the transcendence of the self
may you feel the gentle hug of your soul
wrapped as a cloak all around you.
For we are a body in a soul.
The universe is a creative force.
Wisdom is a journey from imitation to creation.
Creating from true authenticity
is what moves the world forward.
May the divinity of nature always be your guide.
We are connected to everything
and are connected with everything.
May you greet the mystery of the unknown
as you surrender to the journey.
God shows up in us as us.
Give and so you shall receive
for what you seek is seeking you.
May the expansion of presence greet you
as the bliss of moments.
For joy exists in the here and the now.
We are love.
May you come home to love
as the Cuoreosity of your own arrival
swallows you whole.

About the Author

 Jamie Millard is a proud Canadian of Greek, Celtic, and Anglo-Saxon descent. He resides in London, Ontario. A physiotherapist by craft he has spent his life as an empathic healer and hope dealer. Jamie has compassionately served the people in his community for over thirty years assisting them in overcoming their challenges with pain. Jamie is a student of all things divinely human connection; the purest form of art. Jamie is a communication coach.

A passionate bard celebrating the magic of expression, his quest as laid out by Rilke has always been to "Live the questions". The questions that have no right to go away. The questions that deal with who we are becoming. Poetry is a deeper conversation with our soul as it intersects with the frontiers of our unique humanity. We are after all a body in a soul. Writing in the sweet mystical darkness of early dawn, Jamie is a creative alchemist who enjoys casting lyrical spells on the magical wings of words as the sun slowly kisses the moon.

Printed in Great Britain
by Amazon

32835046R00059